Origins

Hamster Rampage

Anthony McGowan ✳ Jonatronix

OXFO
UNIVERSITY

Map of London

Natural History Museum

London Dungeon

London Eye

Big Ben

3

Chapter 1 – **Stowaway**

"Come on you lot! Hurry up or we'll miss the train," called Ant's mum.

The children were very excited. As a special treat, Ant's mum and dad were taking them to London.

"I want to see all the museums," said Ant. "The Natural History Museum has some amazing dinosaur bones."

"I want to go to the London Dungeon and see all the scary stuff," said Tiger.

"I'd like to see Big Ben," said Cat.

"I'd like to go on the London Eye," said Max.

Max warned the others not to use their watches to shrink. London was a big city. He did not want any of them getting lost.

"And one more thing …" he started to say.

X 7

But Max did not say any more because at
that moment Cat squealed. "Eeeeeek! What's
that, Ant?" she said.

"That ... oh, nothing," said Ant.

A little furry nose peeped out of Ant's trouser pocket.

"You've brought Pickles, haven't you?" said Max.

"Shhhh," whispered Ant. "Don't tell Mum and Dad. They will take us home. I just thought Pickles would like to see London, too!"

Chapter 2 – **Sight seeing**

The children had a great time seeing the sights of London. It was a bit of a rush, but they visited all the places they wanted to see. Ant took photographs using the camera in his watch.

First they went to the Natural History Museum.

Then they went to the London Dungeon.

And then they went to see Big Ben.

Chapter 3 – **A hungry hamster**

After they had seen Big Ben, they walked across a big bridge. Ant's mum bought them each an ice cream.

Ant got Pickles out of his pocket for some fresh air.

"Maybe Pickles wants some ice cream?" said Tiger.

Before Ant could stop him, Tiger stuck his finger into his ice cream then held it out for Pickles to lick. The hamster gobbled up the ice cream greedily.

"Look! He likes it!" said Cat.

"It might make him sick!" said Max.

"Yeah!" said Ant. "That's enough, Tiger."
Ant pulled Pickles away. As he did so, some
of Tiger's ice cream dripped on to Ant's watch.
There was a fizzing noise. Then a beam of
green light shot out towards the hamster.

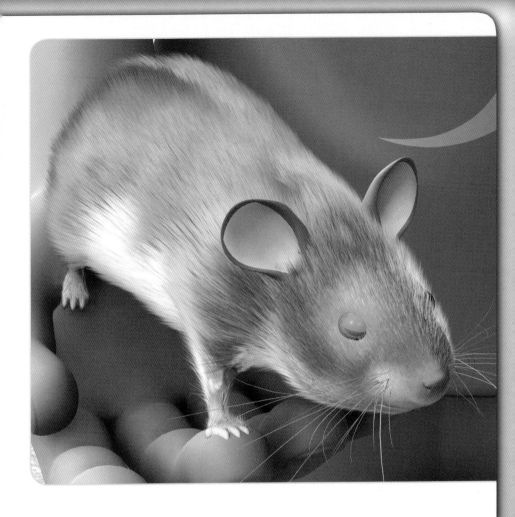

"What was that?" gasped Tiger.

"I don't know," Ant replied.

"Is Pickles OK?" asked Cat.

Ant stared into his eyes. They looked green.

"I'm not sure," said Ant.

"He looks a bit podgy," said Max. "No more ice cream for you today, Pickles!"

Chapter 4 – **Bigger and bigger**

The last treat of the day was a ride on the London Eye. They walked towards it.

"You're right about Pickles putting on weight, Max," said Ant. "He can hardly fit in my pocket."

Ant had to take Pickles out of his pocket and hold him in both hands.

"He looks more like a kitten than a hamster!" laughed Tiger.

"Quick," said Max, "hide him in my bag before your parents see him."

But Pickles grew bigger and bigger.

Ant's parents went to buy tickets for the ride. The children hid the bag behind them.

"Stay here," said Ant's dad. "And don't get into any trouble."

"OK," the children all said, sweetly.

Behind them, they heard a ripping noise.

"Oh, no!" yelped Cat. "Pickles is still growing!"

"He's the size of a bike!" said Tiger.

"He's the size of a car!" exclaimed Ant.

"He's the size of a bus!" said Max.

A lady in the crowd saw Pickles and began to scream. People turned and looked.

Pickles looked around too. He was scared. He saw the London Eye. It was like the hamster wheel in his cage at home. He galloped towards it and jumped up. He ran around the wheel, making it spin very fast.

"Poor Pickles!" wailed Ant.

"Poor people, more like," said Tiger.

The people inside looked terrified.

Chapter 5 – **A giant problem**

"What shall we do?" said Ant.

"There's only one thing we can do," said Max. "Remember what happened with Woody, the stick insect? One of us has to hold on to Pickles and then use their watch to shrink."

"OK," said Cat. "How exactly do we grab hold of a giant hamster on a giant wheel?"

"We need to tempt him down," said Ant.

"What about using ice cream?" Max suggested. "We know he loves that."

"It would have to be a very *big* ice cream," said Cat.

The children looked at the ice-cream van.

"I've got an idea," said Tiger. He ran over to the ice-cream van.

"Excuse me," said Tiger, in his best polite voice. "Can I borrow this?" He pointed to the big, plastic ice cream near the van.

The man in the van wasn't really listening. He was too busy looking at the giant hamster. He just nodded.

Tiger picked up the giant ice cream and took it to Max.

Chapter 6 – **Yee ha, hamster!**

The wheel was spinning faster and faster. Cat and Ant tried to get the hamster's attention.

"Pickles!" they called out.

Tiger waved the giant ice cream. Pickles looked down and saw it. He stopped running.

People scattered as Pickles jumped off the wheel. Tiger ran away from the crowd. Pickles ran after the ice cream. Max ran after Pickles. He grabbed hold of Pickles's long shaggy fur.

"Got you," said Max, as he jumped on his back.

Pickles realized that something was happening. He began to gallop around. Max had to hold on tight. He was like a cowboy riding a wild horse.

"Quick!" shouted Ant. "Use the watch now!"

Max turned the dial on his watch and …

Pickles was soon back to his normal size.
Max jumped off his back. He turned the dial
on his watch again and grew back.

Ant put Pickles in his pocket, just as his
mum and dad returned with the tickets.
They had missed all the action.

"Oh look," said Mum, "the queue's gone. It means we can go straight on. And Ant, you can bring Pickles with you."

"You mean you ..." said Ant.

"Yes, of course, we knew you'd brought him with you," said Dad. "We're not daft, you know!"

The children had a great time seeing the sights from the top of the London Eye. Pickles hid in Ant's pocket all the way round. He'd had enough excitement for one day.

LONDON NEWS

Giant Hamster or Giant Hoax?

The prime minister today dismissed claims that a giant hamster was on the loose in London. He said that it was, "Just an April Fool's joke". He made no further comment when one reporter pointed out that it was March.

Van Man Makes Millions

A driver of an ice-cream van has made over a million pounds by selling his idea for ice-cream flavoured hamster snacks to a large pet food company.

Find out more ...

For more amazing travel adventures, read *Riding the Waves*

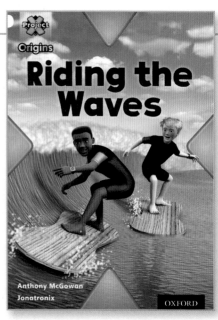

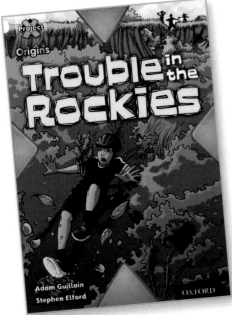

... and *Trouble in the Rockies.*